102 Wacky Monster Jokes

by **Michael Pellowski**

Watermill Press

Library of Congress Cataloging-in-Publication Data

Pellowski, Michael.
      102 wacky monster jokes / by Michael Pellowski.
          p.   cm.
      Summary: A collection of riddles about monsters, including "What
  do monsters like on their mashed potatoes? Grave-y."
      ISBN 0-8167-2746-5 (pbk.)
      1. Wit and humor, Juvenile.   2. Monsters—Juvenile humor.
  [1. Monsters—Wit and humor.   2. Riddles.]   I. Title.   II. Title:
  One hundred two wacky monster jokes.
  PN6163.P444   1992
  818'.5402—dc20   91-44702

What monster tree prowls the forest?

Franken*pine*.

What kind of clothing do monsters wear?

Wash-and-scare clothes.

**What do little monsters like to ride on
at the amusement park?**

The scary-go-round.

What kind of vampire does somersaults?

An acro*bat*.

What did Frankenstein say to his bride?

I've been dying to meet you.

**Why didn't the kids let Dracula play
in the baseball game?**

He kept batting out of turn.

Why is Frankenstein always laughing?

His doctor keeps him in stitches.

What monster nevers loses at games of chance?

Dracu*luck*.

What kind of street do monsters like to live on?

A dead end.

What do you call money given to a monster in exchange for a favor?

The Bribe of Frankenstein.

What monster hibernates in winter?

The *bear*wolf.

What did the doctor say to his monster?

Just be frank around me.

What does a little vampire call his parents?

Mommy and Batty.

What do monsters turn on in the summer?

The scare conditioner.

Why didn't Dracula go to the barbecue?

The hosts were making steaks (stakes).

Who is the messiest monster?

*Slop*zilla.

Why did the mummy get all sticky?

He was wearing gum wrappers.

Where does Judge Dracula work?

Night court.

**What's creepy and leads to the second floor
of a haunted house?**

Mon*stairs.*

When does a monster steer start to howl?

When a bull moon rises.

**What does Dracula wear on his head
when he flies?**

A batting helmet.

Why was the zombie happy to be in court?

He was hoping the judge would give him
a life sentence.

What monster is a rap singer?

Godzilla Ice.

What's woolly and has fangs?

A *Ram*pire.

Who is the brightest monster?

Franken*shine*.

What kind of shoes do ghastly ghouls wear?

Sneaky sneakers.

What vampire whines a lot?

Pout Dracula.

Why did Frankenstein go to a doctor?

He felt stiff all over.

What did one ghoul say to the other?

A fiend in need is a fiend indeed.

What vampire is always eating junk food?

*Snack*ula.

Why did the vampires go into the cave?

To hang out.

What do monsters like to eat with a sandwich?

*Ghoul*slaw.

What's scary and hangs from tree limbs?

Franken*vines*.

Why did the invisible man go on stage?

To perform a vanishing act.

What do you call a twelve-year-old monster?

A Jr. High Ghoul Student.

Why did Dr. Frankenstein go to the mall?

They were having a monstrous sale.

What do you get when Frankenstein pilots a plane?

A terror-flying (terrifying) experience!

**What's spooky and lives on
the bottom of the ocean?**

The Frankenstein *Lob*ster.

How does a lady vampire flirt?

She bats her eyelashes.

What did the mummy detective say?

It's time to wrap up this mystery.

How many parents does a werewolf have?

One maw and four paws.

Why did the werewolf go to bed early?

He was dog-tired.

**What kind of lock does Dracula
have on his door?**

A dead bolt lock.

**What did the critics call
Frankenstein's works of art?**

*Monster*pieces.

What little monster chicken is very creepy?

The Grim Peeper.

**Why did Dracula run out of
the Italian restaurant?**

The chef put garlic on his pizza.

**What did Judge Dracula say to
the coffin at daybreak?**

It's time to close this case.

Why didn't the witch finish her aerobics class?

She wanted to rest a spell.

What did Dracula say to the family counselor?

My kids are driving me batty.

What monster lives in a lumberyard?

*Planken*stein.

What did the mummy say after he was put in aluminum wrap?

Curses! Foiled again!

Who is the richest monster?

Godzillions.

Where do a vampire's designer jeans come from?

*Pant*sylvania.

What has big ears and shrieks?

A haunted mouse.

What did the pharaoh say to the mummy-maker?

Wrap it up. I'll take it home.

Where do monsters go when they have a cold?

To a witch doctor.

**What do you get if you cross a witch
with dynamite?**

A magic boom.

Where does Dracula brush his teeth?

At the *batroom* sink.

What does a monster use to bake bread?

Weird dough (weirdo).

What school did the witch attend?

Charm School.

What do you put in a vampire flashlight?

*Bat*teries.

What's scary and has a long neck?

The Franken*swan* monster.

**What kind of candies do mad doctors
eat after dinner?**

Experi*mints*.

**What do witches have on the floor
of their houses?**

Magic carpeting.

**How do you change a normal doctor
into a mad doctor?**

Don't pay his medical bill.

**What does the abominable snowman wear
on Halloween?**

A ski mask.

Why did the monster have an operation?

To get rid of his *ghoul*stones (gallstones).

Why did Dracula go to a psychologist?

He thought he had bats in his belfry.

Why is Dr. Frankenstein so silly?

His monster scared the wits out of him.

**Who is the most famous vampire hunter
in North America?**

The President of the United Stakes.

Why was the ghoul so sad?

He had grave problems.

Which little monster organization sells cookies?

The Ghoul Scouts.

Why is Dracula's hair messy?

He can't look into a mirror to comb it.

How did the cowboy vampire get dirty teeth?

He kept biting the dust.

Where does a ghoul keep his money?

In a vault.

Does the abominable snowman have dandruff?

Yes. His fur is always covered with flakes.

What is Dracula's favorite racket sport?

*Bat*minton (badminton).

What did the tired zombie say?

I'm dead on my feet.

What hit movie did Michael J. Dracula star in?

Bat to the Future.

What horror movie did Simple Simon star in?

*Pie*day the 13th.

**Where does a monster go when he needs help
writing a composition?**

To a grammar school.

What do you get if you cross a large vampire with someone who gets hairy when the moon is full?

A Big Bat Wolf.

What has fangs and turns on at night?

A *lamp*ire.

Why does Mrs. Werewolf like full moons?

That's when she gets to show off her fur coat.

What monster has spiked hair and radical clothes?

Dracoola.

What monster likes to bowl?

The *spare*wolf.

What do you use to measure a monster?

A graveyard stick.

What's one thing vampires can never be?

Red-blooded citizens.

How do you know if a vampire is on a diet?

He doesn't bite your neck, he just nibbles on it.

What did the mad doctor say to his dumb monster?

Someday I'm going to brain you!

What do monsters like on their mashed potatoes?

Grave-y.

**Why did the monster's ghoulfriend
break up with him?**

Because he was a real creep.

What is Frankenstein's favorite color?

Shocking pink.

What kind of monster tells a lot of fibs?

A vamp*liar*.

What monster lives in a hen-house in Transylvania?

Count *Cluck*ula.

What do you say after you shoot a werewolf with a silver bullet?

Doggone!

Why should you never tell monster jokes?

They're all killers.

Why didn't the Pharaoh ever leave home?

He was tied to his mummy's apron strings.

**What did the bat say to the sheriff
who tried to shoot him?**

Ha! Ha! You just winged me!

Why did the vampire lose his job?

He kept taking days off.

What farm monster feeds the pigs?

Franken*slop*.

Why did Dracula buy a notebook?

He was going to night school.